TRAINING
~ FOR ~
REIGNING

T0015956

TRAINING
～ FOR ～
REIGNING

Releasing the
Power of
Your Potential

Dr. Bill Winston

HIGHERLIFE
PUBLISHING & MARKETING
Oviedo, Florida

Training for Reigning: Releasing the Power of Your Potential by Dr. Bill Winston

Published by HigherLife Development Services, Inc.
PO Box 623307
83 Geneva Drive
Oviedo, Florida 32762
(407) 563-4806
www.ahigherlife.com

ISBN 13: 978-1-954533-82-0
ISBN 10: 1-935245-27-9

Cover Design: Judith McKittrick Wright

March 2022 cover
3 4 5 6 7 - 26 25 2423 22
Printed in the United States of America

Table of Contents

Table of Contents

INTRODUCTION

PEOPLE TODAY TALK ABOUT having it all, getting a piece of the pie. Everybody's talking about living the good life. But what is the good life?

The Bible teaches us that the good life is eternal life. Eternal life isn't meant to start when you get to heaven. It can start today, on this planet when you live your life on the earth like you would if you were in heaven. Eternal life is the life God originally designed for you to live—that's the good life.

Jesus walked on this earth with the purpose of bringing eternal life to the lost and training us to reign with Him. The things that He did and said were structured around and pointed back to the kingdom of God. He encouraged us to pray, "Thy kingdom come, Thy will be done in earth, as it is in heaven" (Matt. 6:10).

Jesus got a handful of people and changed regions one at a time by the power of the Holy Spirit working through them. He is still changing regions one at a time with a handful of people—and He wants to use you! He wants to tap your potential. Perhaps you've had bad experiences in the past and now you're a little shy about stepping out. I'm here to help you conquer that fear.

Expect more from yourself than what you did in the past because your potential is there, waiting to be used. Before you turn to the next page, I want you to say, "Hey, I am not going to leave this earth with all this potential inside of me. Lord, let Your kingdom come in my life here on earth this day, as it is in heaven." Now, let's turn the page together and find out what it means to reign with Christ.

CHAPTER ONE

REIGN OVER YOUR ENEMY

HAVE YOU EVER STEPPED out to do something for God and met resistance? Perhaps you were slapped down so hard that you didn't have a lot of ambition to get up again. That happens. And part of the reason that happens is that we forget that we have an enemy. Anyone in the military will tell you that if you're going to win the battle in front of you, you must know the character, position, and history of your enemy you're about to engage.

So in order for us to reign with Christ, we need to know our enemy. I want to explain that the Bible tells us to watch out for the devil—he's looking for a way to devour you.

> **Be sober, be vigilant; because your
> adversary the devil, as a roaring lion,
> walketh about, seeking whom he
> may devour: Whom resist stedfast
> in the faith, knowing that the same
> afflictions are accomplished in your
> brethren that are in the world. (1 Pet.
> 5:8-9).**

Notice that your brothers and sisters who are reigning beside you have also experienced this adversary. You are not alone!

One of the devil's favorite tactics is to magnify your weaknesses so that you're looking at yourself and your shortcomings instead of your God-given potential. If the devil can get you or someone close to you talking about your weaknesses all the time, you will never get into your potential. You'll take it with you to the grave.

Know Your Enemy

Remember, the devil doesn't have any real power. If he had real power, he'd just kill you! So he tries to keep us in the darkness of lies and ignorance. He wants us to agree with his lies.

> **My people are destroyed for *lack* of knowledge. (Hosea 4:6a, emphasis added)**

Lucifer, or the devil, tries to act like he is fighting against God. God is Lucifer's creator. For The Creator to fight his creation would be demeaning. The creation is no match for its creator. God takes a human being and puts him or her into the world and gives that person faith to deal with the devil.

Jesus said He's going to sit at the right hand of the Father until His enemies are made His footstool.

> **But this man, after he had offered one sacrifice for sins forever, sat down on**

the right hand of God; From hence-forth expecting till his enemies be made his footstool. (Heb. 10:12-13)

Here's the message: as you and I are here representing the kingdom of heaven and depending on Him (our King), the light of God comes in and no longer can the enemy accentuate our weakness. Instead, we can now be used as a sign and a wonder to demonstrate that the world we see is not all there is, that there is a greater reality than the one mankind is living in.

The world has standards by which they live, but as a child of God you are on a higher plane than people in this world. You're on a higher plane than your enemy! God deals with you on the level of the eternal where man was first created, in the God-class, and according to His divine plan for your life.

No one wants to sit in darkness all day and all night. In fact, even as you read this book right now, I declare from this day, you will no longer allow your environment, your circumstances, or your upbringing to keep you at a low level of existence. My purpose for writing this book is to extend my hand to you right now and lift you up to become everything glorious that God has predestined for you to be.

Faith Declares the Outcome before the Fight Starts

The Bible tells us that if we're going to do anything for God, we're going to meet resistance.

We are wrestling principalities, powers, and spiritual wickedness. So, whenever you try to expand the kingdom, a battle is going to be necessary because the enemy is trying to hold the ground that he thinks he owns. Here's the truth: he has been spoiled, stripped of everything that he thought was his, and Jesus (glory to God!) has triumphed over him.

So guess what? You always win. You always win because Jesus has already given you the victory.

> **And this is the confidence that we have in him, that, if we ask any thing according to his will, he heareth us: And if we know that he hear us, whatsoever we ask, we know that we have the petitions that we desired of him. (1 John 5:14-15)**

You see, many times people think that God will give them a vision without provision, but that is against the nature of God. He would not frustrate us like that. What we need to do is understand that our provision will come from the same realm that our vision came from. Remember, every kingdom blessing is first received spiritually before it is delivered practically. So when there is a good fight of faith, that faith has a characteristic to it. It always declares the outcome before the fight ever starts. I think that bears repeating—faith always declares the outcome before the fight ever starts.

Let's just look at what I'm talking about in 1 Samuel, chapter seventeen. Before David became the king of Israel, he met resistance. David was a man who was training for reigning. And what did David do? David declared seven times what he was going to do with Goliath before he ever got to the front line! I've added the numbers to the scriptures so you can easily find the seven declarations.

> **1. Thy servant slew both the lion and the bear: and this uncircumcised Philistine shall be as one of them, seeing he hath defied the armies of the living God.**
>
> **2. David said moreover, The LORD that delivered me out of the paw of the lion, and out of the paw of the bear, he will deliver me out of the hand of this Philistine. (1 Sam. 17:36-37)**

3. Then said David to the Philistine, Thou comest to me with a sword, and with a spear, and with a shield: but I come to thee in the name of the LORD of hosts, the God of the armies of Israel, whom thou hast defied. This day will the LORD deliver thee into mine hand;

4. and I will smite thee,

5. and take thine head from thee;

6. and I will give the carcases of the host of the Philistines this day unto the fowls of the air, and to the wild beasts of the earth; that all the earth may know that there is a God in Israel.

7. And all this assembly shall know that the LORD saveth not with sword and spear: for the battle is the LORD's, and he will give you into our hands (1 Sam. 17:45-47).

Do you see that? David declared what he was going to do to Goliath before he ever got to the front line. Don't wait till you get in the fight to declare something. Start declaring it before the fight ever takes place. And you'll find that your declaration is at least seventy percent of the battle that you're going to fight. Your declaration really is the most important part of your victory. Let's look at another situation where the declaration preceded the victory.

> **And the same day, when the even was come, he saith unto them, Let us pass over unto the other side (Mark 4:35).**

Jesus said to them, "Let us go over to the other side." Now some people think that what He was simply saying was, "Let's go over to the other side." And that's true...but He was also making a declaration. He was declaring the victory. You see, once Adam sinned, part of Adam's sight was lost. It's called *revelation* or *discernment*. Revelation is advanced knowledge from God. Jesus had a full spectrum of reality. Adam could see this natural world and he could also look into the unseen world. Adam could see things and Jesus could see things. Jesus taught His disciples to pray the Father and He would show them things to come. So Jesus knew there would be demonic resistance as they journeyed across to the other side, but He decreed it and fell asleep as the disciples began the journey. He said, "We are going over to the other side." Praise God! And they succeeded in their journey.

Now, let's look at one more example of the way that Jesus always declared the outcome before the fight ever started.

> Now a certain man was sick, named Lazarus, of Bethany, the town of Mary and her sister Martha. (It was that Mary which anointed the Lord with ointment, and wiped his feet with her hair, whose brother Lazarus was sick.) Therefore his sisters sent unto

**him, saying, Lord, behold, he whom
thou lovest is sick. When Jesus heard
that, he said, This sickness is not unto
death, but for the glory of God, that
the Son of God might be glorified
thereby. Now Jesus loved Martha, and
her sister, and Lazarus. When he had
heard therefore that he was sick, he
abode two days still in the same place
where he was. (John 11:1-6)**

A runner came to Jesus from the house of
Lazarus where Jesus often stayed when He
went into that part of the country. He ran
up to Jesus and His disciples and said, "Hey,
your friend Lazarus is sick. Come quickly."
Well, Jesus stayed there two more days. Why?
Because Jesus is not moved by circumstance—
He is moved by what He believes and what the
Father has spoken. Jesus made some statements:

**Our friend Lazarus sleepeth; but I go,
that I may awake him out of sleep.
Then said his disciples, Lord, if he**

sleep, he shall do well. Howbeit Jesus spake of his death: but they thought that he had spoken of taking of rest in sleep. Then said Jesus unto them plainly, Lazarus is dead. And I am glad for your sakes that I was not there, to the intent ye may believe; nevertheless let us go unto him. (John 11:11-15)

The original Greek does not say, "Lazarus is dead." Jesus never said he was dead; Jesus didn't call people dead. He said, "He died." He's not dead—he died. Do you hear the difference? Jesus confessed the victory before He ever got to Lazarus.

When we're in the battle, we must watch our mouths—especially when the pressure is on. The reason why the enemy puts pressure on you is because he's trying to get you to have more faith in your circumstances than you do in God's Word. Are you following what I'm saying? And the time when that confession is most valuable is when you're in the middle of the battle. You have to keep saying what God said. Let's see what happened next in this story.

> Then said Martha unto Jesus, Lord, if thou hadst been here, my brother had not died. But I know, that even now, whatsoever thou wilt ask of God, God will give it thee. Jesus saith unto her, Thy brother shall rise again. Martha saith unto him, I know that he shall rise again in the resurrection at the last day. Jesus said unto her, I am the resurrection, and the life: he that believeth in me, though he were dead, yet shall he live: And whosoever liveth and believeth in me shall never die. Believest thou this? She saith unto him, Yea, Lord: I believe that thou art the Christ, the Son of God, which should come into the world. (John 11:21-27)

Now I want you to watch Jesus's response to Martha. Martha said to him, "I know that he will rise again in the resurrection at the last day." Jesus said to her, "I am..." Wait a minute. Now, there's a powerful revelation right there. Jesus said what? First, He said, "I am." He had to say, "I am," because there is no future where you and I came from. We were born again from above, from heaven's atmosphere. There is no time where we came from. Everything is *now*. "I AM," is the same thing He told Moses when Moses asked God, "Who shall I say sent me?" God answered, "Tell them, I AM hath sent you" (Exod. 3:14).

I AM The Alpha.

I AM The Omega.

I AM The Beginning.

I AM The End.

I AM The Resurrection.

I AM The Life.

Jesus was saying, "When you get Me, you get the past, present, and future." He was saying to Martha, "I don't need to wait until the end to raise him up. *I AM* the end." Are you following what I'm saying?

Let's apply this to you and me right now, today. We don't need to wait until payday to get a paycheck. I AM is running the kingdom! The fallen man has to wait until payday because he's subdued by the natural progression of time, but faith takes us above the restrictive limitation of time. Faith enables us to bring things into the now. And the force of faith is launched in words. Once you come into faith, faith always wins, and faith brings it into where you want it to be.

I want you to say this right now: "I decree I'll never be broke another day in my life." My friend, when you believe and speak in faith, the whole universe will adjust if necessary to fulfill your demands.

State Your Faith, Then Shut Your Mouth

Let's look at another story about Jesus and how He declared his future. The Word of God is so alive to us today. Let's look at the story of Jairus:

> **And, behold, there cometh one of the rulers of the synagogue, Jairus by name; and when he saw him, he fell at his feet, And besought him greatly, saying, My little daughter lieth at the point of death: I pray thee, come and lay thy hands on her, that she may be healed; and she shall live. (Mark 5:22-23)**

Notice that Jairus fell at Jesus' feet. Now, understand, he did this publicly, which wasn't a good idea because Jesus was not that popular. Why? Because of those religious boys! They wanted him out of there. The poor people wanted Jesus—they heard him gladly—but not those religious rulers. Why? Because they had set up their religious traditions, and when you come in preaching the truths of the kingdom of God, denominational folks don't quite want to hear that. Historically there have been a lot of divisions in the body of Christ because of our denominational concepts; however, teaching of the kingdom of God unites.

So Jesus went with Jairus to minister to his little girl.

> And Jesus went with him; and much people followed him, and thronged him. And a certain woman, which had an issue of blood twelve years, And had suffered many things of many physicians, and had spent all that she had, and was nothing bettered, but rather grew worse, When she had heard of Jesus, came in the press behind, and touched his garment. For she said, If I may touch but his clothes, I shall be whole. And straightway the fountain of her blood was dried up; and she felt in her body that she was healed of that plague. And Jesus, immediately knowing in himself that virtue had gone out of him, turned him about in the press, and said, Who touched

my clothes? And his disciples said unto him, Thou seest the multitude thronging thee, and sayest thou, Who touched me? And he looked round about to see her that had done this thing. But the woman fearing and trembling, knowing what was done in her, came and fell down before him, and told him all the truth. And he said unto her, Daughter, thy faith hath made thee whole; go in peace, and be whole of thy plague. (Mark 5:24-34)

Jesus starts to go with Jairus and here comes this lady. She has had an issue of blood for twelve years, and she began to say, "If I can just touch his clothes… If I can just touch His clothes, I shall be whole." And what does she do? She pressed her way through that crowd and touched his garment. Pow! Virtue flowed. The anointing removed burdens, destroyed yokes, and she felt in her body that she was healed of that plague.

Jesus said, "Who touched me?"

The disciples said, "All these people pushing on you."

He said, "No, somebody—somebody touched me."

You see, if you really want something from Jesus, you can draw it out whenever and wherever you need to. I mean, you can be in a crowd, but if you've got your faith together and you came to the meeting to get something that you refuse to leave without, God will turn the man of God to minister right to your need, operating through the Holy Spirit and God's representatives.

I've had this happen to me while I'm preaching at meetings. I can be preaching right along a particular line, and all of a sudden I will change my subject matter and start preaching on something that I didn't even have in my notes. Understand, God is no respecter of people; He is a respecter of faith.

Jesus just told the woman, "Go your way; your faith has made you whole," and while still speaking, a runner comes from Jairus's house to give Jairus some bad news about his daughter's condition. I'm telling you, the battle is on. Why? Because you're trying to get to the other side.

> **While he yet spake, there came from the ruler of the synagogue's house certain which said, Thy daughter is dead: why troublest thou the Master any further? As soon as Jesus heard the word that was spoken, he saith unto the ruler of the synagogue, Be not afraid, only believe. (Mark 5:35-36)**

Shh, shh, shh. Jesus is telling Jairus, "Do not be afraid, only believe."

Only what? Only believe. Believe what? Believe the word that you said when I first met you! Don't open your mouth against it! Practice the vocabulary of silence.

Jesus is saying, "You released your faith, and faith is working on your behalf. Delays are not denials. You don't have to keep talking. Once faith is released, you can close your mouth and let faith work! Fight the good fight of faith!" Don't even respond to the negative circumstances. "Just keep walking with me," Jesus says."We are going to your house today. You said if I just lay my hands on her that she may be healed and she shall live, then she's going to get up. I don't care what condition she's in." Whatever man cannot repair, God will restore to you today!

My friend, it's never too late in the kingdom!

Look what springs up from the faith of Jairus:

> **And he cometh to the house of the ruler of the synagogue, and seeth the tumult, and them that wept and wailed greatly. And when he was come in, he saith unto them, Why make ye this ado, and weep? the damsel is not**

dead, but sleepeth. And they laughed him to scorn. But when he had put them all out, he taketh the father and the mother of the damsel, and them that were with him, and entereth in where the damsel was lying. And he took the damsel by the hand, and said unto her, Talitha cumi; which is, being interpreted, Damsel, I say unto thee, arise. And straightway the damsel arose, and walked; for she was of the age of twelve years. And they were astonished with a great astonishment (Mark 5:38-42.)

Jairus went by faith to Jesus to heal his daughter and in the end he received his little girl back from the dead! Whatever Satan has done in your life, God will repair it today.

Despise or Honor

There is so much power in what we say. We must be careful that we honor the Lord with the request of our lips and the faith of our heart. There's a story in the book of Numbers that talks about the people of Israel after they escaped Egypt and were marching over wilderness to get to the promised land. They had been getting manna to eat every morning, their daily bread, and they were tired of it. Let's see how God responded to their complaining.

> **And say thou unto the people, Sanctify yourselves against tomorrow, and ye shall eat flesh...Ye shall not eat one day, nor two days, nor five days, neither ten days, nor twenty days; But even a whole month, until it come out at your nostrils, and it be loathsome unto you: because that ye have despised the LORD which is among you, and have wept before him, saying, Why came we forth out of Egypt? (Num. 11:18-20)**

Here's the picture: "that you have despised the Lord, which is among you, and have wept before him, saying, 'Why came we forth out of Egypt?'" (v. 20).

The word *despise* means "to loathe or to regard with contempt; regard as despicable or to have a low opinion of." *People today can despise the Lord by despising His Word.* The opposite of despising the Lord is to honor the Lord, and honoring the Lord has to do with putting weight on what He said versus what your circumstances have dictated.

As children of God, we must honor the Lord and honor His Word. The good news is that if you honor Him, He will honor you.

Do you recall the story of the three Hebrew young people who were caught in the middle of a bad situation? The king told them to bow down to his statue, and what did they say? "The God that we serve, He will deliver us" (Dan. 13:17). That is honoring God. Why? Because God told them in Exodus, chapter twenty, in the Ten Commandments, not to bow down to any other gods. And so, they refused to do it, honoring God's Word and so now God honored them. They were delivered from the fire and promoted.

The book of Daniel tells us that they went into the fire, but what happened? The fire wouldn't burn them. They came out with not even the smell of smoke on them.

We must make sure we honor God in every one of our circumstances. Now, what has the enemy done? The enemy has tried to program us through the world system not to resist his temptations. I heard one person say about "religion" that "religion always puts us in a place of non-resistance." The enemy has tried to train us in unbelief. He is trying to inoculate us. When people get flu shots and vaccinations, they actually are given a little bit of the virus so their bodies will work up enough immunity so that when the flu does come, they won't catch it. Well, that's what the enemy does; he gives people a little dose of something called "religion" so they can work up some resistance to the truth, thinking they have heard it all.

Folks say healing has passed away with the Apostles…you've got to get sick to die. These are statements that come from what one man calls a "genetically altered Bible." They are religious statements that are embalmed with unbelief.

What I'm saying here is that the Bible is a book that was written for us as a contract, a covenant, and a constitution! And if you believe it and practice what it says, no devil in hell has a chance to stop you. If you seek God and you just put more weight on Him than you do on what's politically correct or what your circumstances dictate, that honors Him, and He will honor you. And bless God…no man can honor you quite like God.

Chapter Two

Adopted to Reign

In the United States, we live in a democratic society where our leaders are voted into office. But it's not that way in some countries. You and I know that if a king rules over a country, that king does not ask the people of his kingdom to elect his son or daughter to be the next king or queen. If a king is in charge of a country, then the king's child is the next in line to reign. In fact, oftentimes that child gets to rule in power *with* their father and mother because he or she is part of the royal family. Well, as believers, you and I are children of God. We are new creations, a race of kings, Jesus is the King of Kings and the Lord of Lords (Rev. 19:16).

> **For as many as are led by the Spirit of God, they are sons of God. For ye have not yet received the spirit of bondage again to fear; but ye have received the *Spirit of adoption*, whereby we cry, Abba, Father. The Spirit itself beareth witness with our spirit that we are the children of God. And if children, then heirs, heirs of God, and joint-heirs with Christ; if so be that we suffer with him, that we may be also glorified together. (Rom. 8:14-17, emphasis added)**

> **To redeem them that were under the law, that we might receive the adoption as sons. (Gal. 4:5)**

The Greek translation of the word *adoption* in these verses has nothing to do with somebody outside of the family coming into the family. The word *adoption* here has to do with somebody being adopted into full status in the family. We're talking about mature offspring here, not a baby. This word *adoption* refers to a responsible person who's grown from childhood to adulthood who receives ceremony commencing their full status as an adult, the spirit of adoption. Let's look again:

> **The Spirit itself beareth witness with our spirit that we are the children of God. And if children, then heirs, heirs of God, and joint-heirs with Christ; if so be that we suffer with him, that we may be also glorified together. (Rom. 8:16-17).**

The suffering mentioned here has nothing to do with suffering sickness or suffering some disease. That's not the suffering he is talking about in this verse. We are partakers of *His* suffering, meaning that we have to stand for what Jesus died to provide when He suffered on the cross. We have to stand against persecution and believe what Jesus taught us. That we can have victory in every situation.

Allow me to share with you another scripture found in Ephesians, chapter two:

> **For by grace are ye saved through faith; and that not of yourselves: it is the gift of God: Not of works, lest any man should boast. For we are his workmanship, created in Christ Jesus unto good works, which God hath before ordained that we should walk in them. (Eph. 2:8-10)**

Here's verse ten in the Amplified version of the Bible. Just look at this!

> **For we are God's [own] handiwork (His workmanship), recreated in Christ Jesus, [born anew] that we may do those good works which God predestined (planned beforehand) for us [taking paths which He prepared ahead of time], that we should walk in them [living the good life which He**

prearranged and made ready for us to live]. (Eph. 2:10 AMP)

So you see here that God prepared and prearranged things so that you and I can live the good life as an adopted child of God. That's powerful, isn't it? I hope you're beginning to feel how special you are to your Father God! He's prepared things for you and wants you to reign with him.

When that reality of heaven comes in you, then you can decree the will of God into manifestation on earth, in the name of Jesus. As I go into an area, I am supposed to have dominion through the kingdom of God and transform that area into kingdom living.

God didn't prepare you and me to live thinking only in terms of a denomination; He prepared us to live and reign in His kingdom and bring His kingdom of heaven down to the earth. This is being kingdom-minded where we see ourselves as ambassadors, representatives sent from the king, and we are here to enforce

His laws, His values, His principles, and His culture into this foreign land. We are supposed to take everything around us that's out of line with heaven and bring it back into divine alignment. We have been given the authority and kingly anointing to do this because our Father is the King and Lord over all.

The Divine Power Shift

When Jesus came, He really brought a shift in power. He shifted the power away from the Judaism of sacrificing bulls and goats over to the power of the sacrificed Lamb of God. He died for our sins, arose the third day, and took back everything that the enemy had stolen from mankind. Jesus went about preaching and teaching the gospel of the kingdom. The good news about forgiveness and restoration. The scripture tells us Jesus "went about doing good, and healing all that were oppressed of the devil; for God was with him" (Acts 10:38).

The Apostle Paul said,

And my speech and my preaching was not with enticing words of man's wisdom, but in demonstration of the Spirit and of power. (1 Cor. 2:4)

For the kingdom of God is not in word, but in power. (1 Cor. 4:20)

Jesus sent His disciples out and told them to heal the sick and even raise the dead (See Matthew, chapter ten). Now you know, the average funeral that we have today in churches doesn't end like this. If somebody came up during a funeral and spoke to a dead body and the dead body sat up, most of the folks would leave! They would get out in a hurry! And don't let the man speak! If he sits up and speaks, then that would just do it—that would be the end of that service!

So what am I saying? Psalm 66:3 says, "…through the greatness of thy power shall thine enemies submit themselves to thee." We are entering the power era of the Church. We need power to manifest sonship. And until power is on display, release will not come. Power is the principle requirement for total release. We are sent to advance the kingdom, and real advancement does not come without power. "For the kingdom of God is not in word but in power" (1 Cor. 4:20).

Born Again into God's Kingdom

In John, chapter three, we see a man named Nicodemus who came to Jesus by night. Nicodemus asked Jesus, "How can you do all these things?"

Jesus said, "You must be born again."

Most folks look at being born again as some kind of religious thing, but being born again has nothing to do with religion. If a person is born again, they become a Christian and Christianity is not a religion, it is a family. If you are born again and brought into the family of God, then you become a citizen of heaven and you now have certain rights.

Let's look at it this way. People in the church many times are born again and they choose to stand just inside the door of the kingdom—but they've never come all the way inside the kingdom to find out how the kingdom operates and what in fact belongs to them. So they stand at the door like a servant, but do not enter like a son. In fact, people are oftentimes ignorant of their privileges and also their responsibilities.

What did Jesus teach? Jesus said that you're in the world but not of the world. That means that you and the world are speaking two different languages.

Jesus answered, My kingdom is not of this world. (John 18:36a)

I got out my *Strong's Concordance of the Bible* and looked up *world* from this passage in John.* *Strong's Concordance* says that the word

---

* James Strong, *Strong's Exhaustive Concordance of the Bible* (Peabody, MA: Hendrickson Publishers, 2007), entry 2889.

world comes from the word *cosmos*, having to do with the order or arrangement of things.

You see, our enemy is Satan and he stole the authority of the world from Adam. Because the enemy took charge of the world, we do not have the order of heaven here anymore. The enemy brought chaos.

Somebody may say, "Well it looks pretty orderly to me." If we look close enough and compare our world today with heaven, we'll see an absence of truth and a host of other things that do not exist in heaven:

- Lawlessness
- Injustice
- Poverty
- Sickness
- Disease
- Premature death
- Disasters
- Toiling and sweating trying to make ends meet

- Demonic forces and dominions
- Hatred
- Jealousy
- Racism
- Deception

All of this is chaotic and that's what's been in this earth. No wonder Jesus told us to pray:

Thy kingdom come, Thy will be done in earth, as it is in heaven. (Matt. 6:10)

So what happened? He chose you. He chose you to join His family, and now He is training you so that He can send you out and you can rule wherever He sends you. That means that every place the sole of your foot will tread upon you will bring under kingdom jurisdiction and divine order. You have a superior attitude, an attitude of love and service, not pride and bitterness. You have a superior power working for you that will bring everything that is out of line with the kingdom of God into divine alignment. So it's your time! God has called you for such a time as this, and He is sending you forth!

Righteousness—The Key to Reigning

Righteousness is a key to why many people have not entered into this lifestyle of reigning with Christ. What is righteousness? Righteousness is not conduct or the way you act—that's holiness. Righteousness is the nature of the Father imparted to us so that we are put in right standing with God. Of course, if you're born of God, His nature is going to come right out of you. Being righteous means the ability to stand in the presence of the Father God without the sense of guilt or inferiority or shame. Righteousness:

- restores dominion
- restores fellowship
- restores peace

- restores freedom
- restores your faith.

Once righteousness comes, faith flows like a flood. You have been made the righteousness of God in Him. You have rights. Your inheritance, that which God has given you, always comes in proportion to this new identity. You are in a new family! You have new authority! Now we must be trained to reign.

There are standards out there, and we have been trained in those standards. This world we live in does things a certain way, almost completely opposite from the kingdom. But once you come into the family of God, you have a whole different standard by which you should live in this society. This new standard will distinguish you. The Bible says that the unsaved will see you and acknowledge that you are the righteous planting of God, a holy people. They will be able to spot you anywhere. They will readily identify you as a righteous man or woman.

The Bible says in the book of Revelation that there is no crying in heaven. I don't have to cry anymore.

Jesus said, "My peace I give unto you" (John 14:27). This is not the kind of peace that the world gives you, because they don't have peace.

The joy of the Lord is ours! I'm talking about joy that comes from heaven. I can be full of joy all the time. I don't need to be up one day and down the next.

Faith makes it so we can live on earth just like it is in heaven. No sickness, no poverty, no shame, guilt, disappointments, or failures. It's ours right now. You have a right to say, "I'll never be sick another day in my life."

I know this may feel strange, but just say these words out loud right now: "I will never be sick another day in my life."

Someone might say that doesn't make sense. Well, it's not designed to make sense. It's designed to make faith. In the kingdom, you declare the outcome before you ever enter the battle! Heaven is our inheritance! We sing about heaven, we talk about heaven, but we can have heaven right here and now. Didn't Jesus tell us to pray this way: "Thy kingdom come, Thy will be done in earth, as it is in heaven"? Let people see how good your God is! Show them how good heaven is! This is your inheritance! It's written right into your adoption papers!

Chapter Three

The Power of Potential

What is *POTENTIAL*? Potential is *hidden abilities*. It's something that is already there that you have not yet become. That's potential. Who placed potential in you? Where did your potential come from? It came from God. It came from the one who made you, created you and designed you. He put inside you all that it takes to be fruitful, multiply, and replenish the earth. And just as the manufacturer tests the product before putting it on the market, God tested you in heaven before you were delivered on earth. Every other test result contrary to that is a satanic lie.

Perhaps you're wondering, *Well, OK, it's in there, but how does potential come out?* This is an amazing thing, and I hope you can understand what this looks like. Potential is fulfilled by placing a demand on it. Potential needs a demand—it just doesn't ooze out of you with nothing to do, but it needs a demand. So what we are saying here is that if potential is to be released, it needs a demand and if you don't put a demand on potential, you'll die with it—but the potential is still in there.

This is God's way in training for reigning. He wants us to go beyond those things that are easily attainable. He wants us to step out of the boat and go further because He's got a lot of potential locked up inside each and every one of us. He wants you maybe to try things that you've never done before or to experience a wealth that is already inside of you. If you step out and take the responsibility He's offering you, God will give some ability to help you in your responsibility. Expect more from yourself than things that can easily be in your reach.

I said this in the introduction of this book, but it bears repeating. We need to take the leap of faith, be willing to risk what we think may be a failure, and say, "Hey, I am not going to die with all this potential inside of me." OK? And remember, your true ability cannot be measured. No IQ test can measure your potential. I decree, whatever God has planned for your life on this earth you will accomplish it.

Potential Like Adam

Even within the perfect environment of the Garden of Eden, God placed a demand on Adam so that Adam would come forth with his potential. God told Adam to name the animals. Before Adam was created, God spoke things into existence. He did not speak Adam into existence. Adam was made to be an extension of God, the image of God. The Bible calls him in Luke, "the son of God."

Which was the son of Enos, which was the son of Seth, which was the son of *Adam*, which was the son of God. (Luke 3:38, emphasis added)

Just as God operated, Adam was to operate. The Bible calls Jesus the last Adam, so Jesus's actions were to show you and me how Adam really was (1 Cor. 15:45).

Adam was an extension of God and, really, Adam's ability was almost unlimited. I want to try to give you a picture of Adam because if you see Adam, then you're looking into the mirror at your own reflection.

I believe that Adam was born of God and functioned in the glory of God. He didn't have any clothes on and did not need any because he had the covering of the glory.

Adam was supernatural—he didn't function naturally. Adam had normal sight and supernatural insight. He not only saw like we do in a natural, three-dimensional way, but he went to that fourth dimension. He could see on out there. He was made in the image of God. His spirit was dominant over his flesh. Of course, after Adam sinned, his flesh became dominant over his spirit and he functioned basically by seeing through the veil of the curse. But think of this—now God has restored all this to man through Jesus.

Potential Like Jesus

Jesus began to show people how Adam actually functioned. Let's look at what the religious leaders said about Jesus:

> **And the Jews marvelled, saying, How knoweth this man letters, having never learned? Jesus answered them, and said, My doctrine is not mine, but his that sent me. (John 7:15-16)**

You can see that the religious leaders were kind of confused. They were saying, "How does he know so much when he hasn't been trained?" (John 7:15b, NLT).

In the Gospels, Jesus is called the only begotten Son of God. Have you heard that before? But after the Gospels He is not called the only begotten Son of God, He is called the Firstborn and in one place He's called the Firstborn of many brethren (Rom. 8:29). In Hebrews, He's called the Firstborn of the church (Heb. 12:23). Why are they calling him "firstborn"? Doesn't first indicate there's a second somewhere in the world? He is preeminent. He is the head. He's the one that's first, so we call him Lord, the Lord of Lords. We call him King, the King of Kings.

Remember that Jesus, once He was raised from the dead, had a glorified body. He said "Handle me, put your fingers in the holes of my hand, put your hand in my side, check me out, see that I am flesh and bone." He didn't say anything about blood, because the blood was shed for us. I believe that in the beginning Adam had the glory running through his veins.

> **And after six days Jesus taketh Peter, James, and John his brother, and bringeth them up into an high mountain apart, And was transfigured before them: and his face did shine as the sun, and his raiment was white as the light. (Matt. 17:1-2)**

His face did shine as the sun and his raiment was white as the light. Adam was covered with light. Now I want you to see this because we're getting back to the glory. See, Jesus came to restore the years that the cankerworm had taken away.

My point to you is that you've got to come up to the divine nature of God. You've got to be who God says you are, and any man that's in Christ is a brand new species of being. You are something that never has hit this earth before! You just happen to have your old body on the covering of it, but you've got something new and powerful under the cover.

The enemy doesn't want you to understand this because he's using that to try to keep the body of Christ from the eternal—because he knows that with that comes power. What kind of power? The kind of power that will convert the most terrorizing terrorist. The kind of power that will stop a storm. That's the kind of power I'm talking about! The kind of power that will give proof that Jesus is Lord!

This is your time and it's all in your potential! It's locked up in there right now and God wants it exposed. You are an extension of Him. Look at Jesus, look at Adam. God was light, so was Adam. Adam worked the garden by faith and Jesus worked the harvest of this world by faith. People told Jesus, "We don't have enough to feed them."

Jesus replied, "Yes you do. There's a boy there with a two-piece fish dinner. Bring it here." What did He do? Jesus looked up, blessed it, and it started multiplying (John 6:9-11). You need to renew your mind because Adam had the full scope of his mind to use. Adam had the mind of God and now through Jesus we have the mind of Christ. Adam could name animals just as quickly as God could, because he and God were one!

Place a Demand on Your Potential

Stop thinking you're just somebody stumbling through the earth "trying to make heaven your home." The Bible says you're already seated in heaven, in heavenly places (Eph. 2:6). You're walking in your body in the earth and you're seated with Christ in your spirit in heaven. You're at both places at the same time. You start getting this revelation and you will leave all the petty jealousies and all the strife that has hung people up behind you. You'll set your affections on things above. Having a billion dollars to you won't be any different from having one hundred dollars because the true riches are in the anointing.

God is speaking to you right now as you're reading this book. He's saying, *OK, get out of the boat, place a demand on that anointing! Let's make that potential come out.* It's time to expose who you really are and who He really is.

My Lord, the devil's so scared that you're going to come out and discover who you are because all of a sudden you're going tell him where to go, and tell those demons and disease where to go, too.

Think about this. The garden was big. It wasn't some little old garden spot on the north end of town. The rivers indicate how long it was. Some say it was about four thousand miles long and about two thousand miles wide. (That's how long the river was.) That was the garden. Adam couldn't walk all the way over that garden! That would take him days! So how could he move? I believe he moved at the speed of thought.

Don't say what you can't do because you have a flesh and blood body. Jesus did it! He had a flesh and blood body. He walked on water. Then he invited Peter to do the same, challenging the great potential hidden inside us.

The Kingdom Diet

I want to look at Scripture that tells the story of Daniel. Daniel and his three friends were young teenagers when Nebuchadnezzar of Babylon took Judah into captivity.

> **But Daniel purposed in his heart that he would not defile himself with the portion of the king's meat, nor with the wine which he drank: therefore he requested of the prince of the eunuchs that he might not defile himself. (Dan. 1:8)**

I'm pointing this out because we have to get on a different diet. A denominational diet won't get you there. You have to go on a kingdom diet.

I'm not speaking against people in denominations; I'm just saying we cannot eat traditional denominational food and develop a kingdom mindset.

The eunuch didn't want to do it, but he agreed, and he checked them for ten days to see if, in fact, they'd look weak or what have you. But they looked very strong after they refused to eat the king's meat.

> **As for these four children, God gave them knowledge and skill in all learning and wisdom: and Daniel had understanding in all visions and dreams. Now at the end of the days that the king had said he should bring them in, then the prince of the eunuchs brought them in before Nebuchadnezzar. And the king communed with them; and among them all was found none like Daniel, Hananiah, Mishael, and Azariah: therefore stood they before the king. And in all matters of wisdom**

and understanding, that the king enquired of them, he found them ten times better than all the magicians and astrologers that were in all his realm. (Dan. 1:17-20)

God gave them an endowment of knowledge and skill in all learning and wisdom. Their performance was ten times better than the PhDs, the lecturers, the doctors, the philosophers, the sorcerers, the magicians, the mathematicians, the physicists, and the chemists of that day, in all of Babylon. These young men who were loyal to God excelled in all knowledge and skill and all learning! You've got to believe that God is endowing you so that you will have ten times more knowledge than folks who are naturally in this world. The knowledge that the world has is not good enough to solve the global problems and make it so that people can survive and come through the times that are soon coming.

There is an anointing that is available to the believer for their performance to exceed any ability in the natural, secular, molecular world that you live in. You are just going to know things—not because you have experienced them, but because of God's ability on human flesh to do what only God can do.

Remember that potential is *hidden ability*. It is something that is built in on the inside of you determined by the One who created you. You must place a demand on that potential if it's to be released and manifested in this earth.

How did Daniel and his friends get that ability? They didn't go to school to get it. It came by grace. If God will do that for Daniel and his three friends, then He can endow you today because it is a part of your inheritance as a child of God.

Kingdom Language

I'm not trying to negate education. Bless God, education is supposed to draw out something in you, but I'm telling you in that place of academic learning you're supposed to be ten times better than people outside the covenant with God. Now, you know God can endow you, because look what happened at the Tower of Babel. It's a long story, but the short of it is that God came down because the people were building a tower to reach heaven and God confused and confounded their speech. What did He do? He changed their languages. Now if this does not agree with your theology, look how they supernaturally spoke in languages they had never gone to school to learn in Acts, chapter two.

In Africa right now, you can go twenty miles and one of the tribes there won't even be able to communicate with a tribe that is twenty miles away. Why? Because they speak two different languages. My point to you is: look at what God did! Just in one sweep, He gave them languages they never spent time to learn.

If God can do that with them, then can't He do that with us today? Can't He make it so if you go to Mexico and you don't speak Spanish, that as soon as your feet hit the soil off that airplane you can speak the language? I'll just open my mouth and He will fill it. I mean, this is just the tip of the iceberg. He's infinite. We are endowed with the blessing and giftings that can make us smarter than anybody else.

> **For if by one man's offence death reigned by one; much more they which receive abundance of grace and of the gift of righteousness shall reign in life by one, Jesus Christ. (Rom. 5:17)**

Do you see that word *reign* in there? Let's look at this verse in the Amplified Bible:

> **For if because of one man's trespass (lapse, offense) death reigned through that one, much more surely will those who receive [God's] overflowing**

**grace (unmerited favor) and the free
gift of righteousness [putting them
into right standing with Himself]
reign as kings in life through the one
Man Jesus Christ (the Messiah, the
Anointed One). (Rom. 5:17 AMP)**

God put us in right standing with Him
so that we can "reign as kings in life." That's
royalty—and that's the potential inside of you.

CHAPTER FOUR

QUALIFIED TO REIGN

ARE YOU TRYING TO qualify yourself? Do you find your thoughts arguing back and forth? Don't cave in to discouragement and think, *Well I didn't finish this, or I didn't finish that.* Do you remember when the angel came to Gideon? The angel called Gideon a "mighty man of valor!"

> And the angel of the LORD appeared unto him, and said unto him, The LORD is with thee, thou mighty man of valour. And Gideon said unto him, Oh my Lord, if the LORD be with us, why then is all this befallen us? and where be all his miracles which our fathers told us of, saying, Did not the LORD bring us up from Egypt?

but now the LORD hath forsaken us, and delivered us into the hands of the Midianites. And the LORD looked upon him, and said, Go in this thy might, and thou shalt save Israel from the hand of the Midianites: have not I sent thee? And he said unto him, Oh my Lord, wherewith shall I save Israel? behold, my family is poor in Manasseh, and I am the least in my father's house. And the LORD said unto him, Surely I will be with thee, and thou shalt smite the Midianites as one man. (Judg. 6:12-16)

Gideon said, "Who? Me?"

Right there, he began to disqualify himself. He said, "Wait a minute. You don't know. My family is one of the poorest families in the tribe. I don't have much education. I don't learn easily like most people. I'm the least among my own brethren." You can see that Gideon's view of himself really didn't make any difference to the call of God on his life. God has a plan. He has preprogrammed a marvelous plan for your life. Do you hear what I'm saying to you? And His plan includes you living on earth like you were in heaven. God has no plan for you to be poor or in any way unworthy of your calling.

Moses had a hard time with this message. God said, "Moses, I want you to go back to Egypt and take Israel out of there and set them free."

Moses said, "I can't talk."

God countered, "Who made your mouth?"

The endowment of the kingdom of heaven that is coming on you as you read this book is not only intellectual, but it's practical. God knows how to help you speak. He made your mouth, He will introduce you to persons or groups of people that He wants to talk to, and He will give you the words to speak. You are the conduit to bring God's kingdom to the earth. You cannot qualify yourself for the job—God is the great qualifier and He says, "Who made your mouth? Who created your potential?"

God's free favors profusely abound in your life, my friend. God knew what kind of potential was in Gideon, He knew what kind of potential was in Moses, and He knows what kind of potential is in you!

Blessed to Give

In Christ, we have inherited Abraham as our father. So we are the seed of Abraham, and just like He blessed Abraham, He's gonna bless you! He blessed Abraham and made him very rich with cattle, silver, land, and gold. And these weren't cows with mad cow disease—these were pedigree stocks! The gold was the gold of Ophir, the finest gold there was.

Canaan not only represents your rest, but it represents His best. God has the best now. What is His best? Heaven is God's best and He told us to pray, "Let Your kingdom come and Your will be done in earth, as it is in heaven."

Perhaps these aren't the standards you've been living under. If this feels like it's over your head, I want to encourage you to jump up, grab it by faith, and say, "Hallelujah! It's mine! I'll take the kingdom of heaven, if you please!"

Perhaps you have been living under these standards. There are people who have grasped this message and are experiencing the kingdom of heaven in their homes and in their everyday lives. If that's you, then you must remember that God gave you something good not just so you can just say how good God is (although that's true), but He gave you His kingdom supplies so that you can bless some other people.

God spoke to my heart recently and said, *Son, when are you gonna stop accumulating all those suits?* He got my attention! He spoke to my heart and said, *Give some of your suits away. Give!*

I said, "Lord, have mercy!" I had suits in that closet that I hadn't worn in years. Why let them accumulate dust? Give them away. Well, I did, and it felt good.

Many times our minds have been affected by something other than the Spirit of God, so when His word first comes to us it may not make sense. In a way, that's good. This message of training for reigning will require faith if it's going to go anywhere.

When Jesus came here, He stood up and told a whole group of people in His home town a message of who He was and why He came. He told them exactly what the kingdom of heaven was like and then He told them, "I'm bringing this kingdom to you right now." Let's look at the scripture that Jesus read that day:

> **And he came to Nazareth, where he had been brought up: and, as his custom was, he went into the synagogue on the sabbath day, and stood up for to read. And there was delivered unto him the book of the prophet Esaias. And when he had opened the book, he found the place where it was written, The Spirit of the Lord is**

upon me, because he hath anointed me to preach the gospel to the poor; he hath sent me to heal the broken-hearted, to preach deliverance to the captives, and recovering of sight to the blind, to set at liberty them that are bruised, To preach the acceptable year of the Lord. And he closed the book, and he gave it again to the minister, and sat down. And the eyes of all them that were in the synagogue were fastened on him. And he began to say unto them, This day is this scripture fulfilled in your ears. (Luke 4:16-21)

Jesus was prepared to bring the kingdom of heaven down to the people of the earth and proclaim that this is the acceptable year of the Lord. Let's look at "the acceptable year of the Lord" in the Amplified Bible:

To proclaim the accepted and acceptable year of the Lord [the day when

**salvation, and the free favors of God
profusely abound]. (Luke 4:19 AMP)**

Notice that the free favors of God profusely
abound. Profuse has to do with lavish—with
liberal, extravagant excess. It has to do with
abounding. Jesus said He came that we might
have life more abundantly (John 10:10).

There is a transfer of the wealth that is taking
place now in this end-time church, that's why
there's so much financial preaching of the
gospel. It's what's got to be preached before
Jesus returns. Finances is an end-time message.
The church is sent to dominate the earth. This
dominion cannot be fully realized without the
wealth (Prov. 22:7).

Now, I'm not saying that we go out and say,
"My name is Jimmy. I'll take all you give me,"
and try to take something. That's not the idea.
We transfer it by faith, glory to God. In other
words, if something is extravagant, if something is big that He tells you to do, don't try
to bring it down to a place where you can earn

it by working for a living. Everything that's in the earth belongs to you. Your issue is not money…it's faith. The faith that takes.

You have to understand that the Bible makes it clear that in the end times, the gospel must be preached throughout all the earth. Who has God commissioned to do that? You and me! But sharing the gospel and doing kingdom work takes not only faith but also money. God knows that. So in addition to giving you all spiritual authority, God wants to release to you the financial authority to do what He's called you to do. Chances are you are thinking too small. You're thinking about what you have in the natural and not seeing that God has given you authority and dominion to execute His plans on the earth. So does that mean you go up to unbelieving strangers and ask them to give you the money you need to carry out God's work? Of course not. Guaranteed, Satan is not going to just give you money to finance a war against him. But God does want you to think higher, bigger, to trust Him more to supply all that you need to accomplish His purpose.

God is Extravagant

Over in Proverbs, chapter thirteen, the Bible tells us that the wealth of the sinner is laid up for the just (v. 22). There is provision that has been lying there, and even when God tells us to do something, we look at it and we begin to look at the cost. We bring the cost of this thing down, down, down until we can reasonably figure out how we can work for it or how we can get enough people together to make it happen. Leave it alone! We need to receive what God tells us He's going to do on the level that He gave it to us.

I'm saying that God is lavish; He is extravagant. Your desire for nice things didn't come from you. It is the nature of God in you. Look around the throne of God! There is nothing cheap around there. There is gold. There are diamonds. I'm saying it's time for heaven to come to earth. Now, for you to receive it, you cannot appeal to your senses. Because senses always bring human limitations and you must go beyond your human limitations. Why? God wants you to receive it by grace through faith. Remember, you can't pay for anything that comes out of heaven. God's plan for the church is not for us to hoard things as some people have done in the world, but to be a distribution center for God to eradicate systemic poverty in the world.

You Own the Whole Estate

We are joint heirs with Jesus Christ. That means we are masters over the entire estate.

> Now I say, That the heir, as long as he is a child, differeth nothing from a servant, though he be lord of all. (Gal. 4:1)

> **Now what I mean is that as long as the inheritor (heir) is a child and under age, he does not differ from a slave, although he is the master of all the estate. (Gal. 4:1 AMP)**

Believing is a choice. God said we own the whole estate. Remember, we don't need to try to figure out how this estate is to physically change hands. The only thing I know is that He promised it, and I don't have to work three jobs to try to get enough money to pay for it.

Call for It!

One Wednesday night a man from Africa stood in the pulpit of my church preaching hard. Suddenly, he backed off preaching and turned to me and said, "Pastor, your airplane is in Ecclesiastes, chapter ten." I had shared with him that we were believing for a ministry airplane, not as a toy, but as a tool to lighten the load of our overseas trips.

Of course, I opened my Bible and began to read Ecclesiastes, chapter ten. I read it once and didn't see my airplane. I read it again and didn't see it; I read it again and didn't see it—but soon, the eyes of my understanding were enlightened (opened)…I saw it! It said, "…for a bird of the air shall carry the voice, and that which hath wings shall tell the matter" (Eccl. 10:20).

Somebody with no discernment, someone who doesn't understand how the kingdom works would have thought he was just making fun, or that is was just another scripture. But it wasn't. It was a seed and I received it as such because in the kingdom, "a seed is all you need." I meditated on that verse. "A bird of the air shall carry my voice."

Two weeks before the writing of this book, my airplane came in.

I called for that plane! God heard and delivered! Remember, every blessing in the kingdom is first received spiritually before it is delivered practically.

I'm training for reigning now and so are you! Maybe you will go into a neighborhood to take buildings back for the kingdom—a place for a business or orphanage. Paul writes, "...all things are yours" (1 Cor. 3:21). In Matthew's Gospel, I noticed that the donkey stayed tied up until Jesus called for it (21:2). And your stuff is staying tied up until you call for it even though it legally belongs to you.

Joshua and Caleb said this: "Let us go up at once, and possess it; for we are well able to overcome it" (Num. 13:30). They saw Canaan as legally theirs, as their heritage, and they refused to die without it.

I want you to picture your stuff all tied up— just sitting there waiting for you to call for it. What is it that you need in order to do what God's called you to do? I want to encourage you to take a moment right now and call for the best. Call it in! Call for the best! You're a child of the king, and you are qualified to bring His kingdom down here to earth! And I declare with you, "Loose that donkey, the Lord has need of it!"

CHAPTER FIVE

THE FACE OF POWER

I'M SURE YOU'VE HEARD the saying, "Don't judge a book by its cover." You know that statement can apply to you and me.

It reminds me of a time when I was a teenager and there was this guy who had an automobile. That automobile looked like an old automobile. In those days, when I was young, we did a little drag racing. I remember we went to this place where we could bet some money and have a little drag race. This guy came up to the starting line with a car that didn't look like it could limp down the block. It didn't look like it was much of anything. He pulled that old car up to the starting line, put some money on the line, and took off! He faked out everybody!

If we were smart, all we had to do was look up under the hood and listen. That car was old looking on the outside, but underneath the hood he was running about five hundred horsepower. We didn't realize that the face or sur*face*, which is the outside of a person or thing, can be totally different from the power that lies within. We need to learn that about the face of power. That's why the Word of God says that sometimes we are unaware when we talk to angels. You and I have actually entertained angels, totally unaware that they were angels. We can't always tell there's power inside of a person by looking at the person's face.

Now, that car is just like you coming into your workplace in your suit or your work clothes. You may look or dress like everybody else on the job. People don't know what's up under the hood, but you're in there speaking in tongues! There's power and potential inside of that suit!

My church needed a place to meet and so we bought a mall. It was a faith fight to get the mall. The city administration opposed us and the banks did not immediately cooperate with the purchase, but God gave us the victory. As we were closing on the mall, miracles were happening left and right. One of the lawyers for the village government asked somebody, "Well, who's with him?"

That person answered, "Nobody, I don't think."

A woman lawyer responded. "No. Somebody's with him."

She was talking about what's under the hood. See I have something—I have Someone under the hood (The Holy Spirit). And you can talk to anyone who was here at the time of purchase— the mall wasn't doing very well. Today we use the back of the mall for our ministry, and the front side of the mall is lined with retail businesses. The mall had been in decline when we purchased it, but now it has completely turned around and is prospering.

People will see something and that God is with you. This will create a platform so that you won't have to labor and sweat trying to convince somebody to get saved. You just show them the evidence and they want to get what you have!

There is potential inside of you. All you need to do is to place a demand on it and you're guaranteed to come out in the winner's circle, just like my friend put his money down on the starting line and put a demand on his old-looking car to win that race.

Use Your Equipment

Let's take a look at the word *power* in the Word of God:

> **And he said unto them, It is not for you to know the times or the seasons, which the Father hath put in his own**

power. But ye shall receive power, after that the Holy Ghost is come upon you: and ye shall be witnesses unto me both in Jerusalem, and in all Judaea, and in Samaria, and unto the uttermost part of the earth. (Acts 1:7-8)

Then he answered and spake unto me, saying, This is the word of the LORD unto Zerubbabel, saying, Not by might, nor by power, but by my spirit, saith the LORD of hosts. Who art thou, O great mountain? before Zerubbabel thou shalt become a plain: and he shall bring forth the headstone thereof with shoutings, crying, Grace, grace unto it. (Zech. 4:6-7)

Power is miracle-working ability.

George Washington Carver was a scientist, a Black man, who lived from 1864 to 1943 and joined Booker T. Washington in Tuskegee. George Washington Carver revolutionized the economy of the South by introducing hundreds of uses for the peanut, soybean, pecan, and sweet potato in the place of cotton. Cotton was on the decline at the time and because slavery was over, there was nobody to pick the cotton. The whole South was going into an economic drought. These crops that Carver utilized were used to replenish the soil in the South, so in those years that he was there, Vice President Calvin Coolidge came to see him. Franklin Delano Roosevelt, who was president, came to see him.

It wasn't long until Carver became the confidant and advisor to people like Thomas Edison and Mahatma Gandhi and leaders all over the world. Edison offered him a position with six figures which was huge during that time, and many times Henry Ford tried to get him to join him in Dearborn, Michigan, at Ford Motor

Company. Why? Because Carver had learned how to make rubber out of milkweed.*

He was an extraordinary scientist, educator, and humanitarian. But even more than that, George Washington Carver was a man of faith. I think about all this man gave to our world and contributed to our society and I wonder, *What made him tick?*

Perhaps we can get a peek inside the heart of this man by looking at an old poem he frequently recited at special events where he was asked to speak:

EQUIPMENT

Figure it out for yourself, my lad,
You've all that the greatest of men have had,
Two arms, two hands, two legs, two eyes
And a brain to use if you would be wise.
With this equipment they all began,
So start for the top and say, "I can."

---

* William J. Federer, *America's God and Country Encyclopedia of Quotations* (St. Louis, MO: Amerisearch, Inc., 2000), 94.

Look them over, the wise and great
They take their food from a common plate,
And similar knives and forks they use,
With similar laces they tie their shoes.
The world considers them brave and smart,
But you've all they had when
they made their start.

You can triumph and come to skill,
You can be great if you only will.
You're well equipped for what fight you choose,
You have legs and arms and a brain to use,
And the man who has risen great deeds to do
Began his life with no more than you.

You are the handicap you must face,
You are the one who must choose your place,
You must say where you want to go,
How much you will study the truth to know.
God has equipped you for life, but He
Lets you decide what you want to be.

Courage must come from the soul within,
The man must furnish the will to win.
So figure it out for yourself, my lad.
You were born with all that the great have had,

With your equipment they all began,
Get hold of yourself and say: "I can."
                    —Edgar A. Guest*

Historians tell us that this was George Washington Carver's favorite poem—he quoted it often. And this poem is telling us that we all have potential within us, that the greatest of men and women who ever lived started out life with the same equipment. God equipped us for life, but we must choose to use that equipment and go after the highest potential that we were created for. Everybody knew that Carver loved God and, because he outperformed the scientists and educators of his day, they respected his God. Your supernatural performance is supposed to create a platform sufficient for you to offer your opinion about God.

---

* Written by Edgar A. Guest (1881-1959) and recited by George Washington Carver during a commencement address in Selma, Alabama, May 27, 1942, as reported by Tuskegee Institute.

See, George Washington Carver had something under the hood—and everybody knew it.

If you're going to step out and do what appears to be impossible, you need to know you've got something under the hood. If you have five hundred horsepower underneath that hood, you don't have to worry! It's going to happen! You're going to win that race.

From an Old Book

Don't hold yourself back! Don't try to stay real close to the shoreline so you don't have to get involved in anything that is going to take a challenge or use something on the inside. Give your ability a chance. Expect more from yourself than the things that are easily reached in your life—place a demand on that.

In 1921, George Washington Carver accepted an invitation to address the U.S. Senate Committee of Ways and Means. They gave him ten minutes to speak. He started speaking with such profoundness that the chairman said, "Go ahead, Mr. Carver, your time is unlimited." And Carver spoke for one hour and forty-five minutes. When he was finished, they were confounded and they asked, "Where did you learn all of these things?"

"From an old book," he replied.

"What book?" they asked.

He said, "The Bible."

The senator replied, "Does the Bible say anything about a peanut?"

Mr. Carver said, "No sir, but it does tell you about the God who made the peanut. I asked Him to show me about the peanut and He did."*

George Washington Carver explains that he never took any scientific textbooks into his laboratory. He would just ask God how to perform his experiments. Now, I'm not saying people are not to go to school and get

---

* William J. Federer, *George Washington Carver: His Life and Faith In His Own Words* (St. Louis, MO: Amerisearch, Inc., 2002), 16.

an education—but look at the textbook this brilliant man depended upon! He openly told the United States Senate that God talked to him and testified that God showed him what no other book in the world could show him. We need this challenge right now! We need to know that the only one that can educate us on this level is the Holy Ghost.

Are You Ready?

I hope you've been blessed and challenged as you've turned these pages. God has placed amazing potential on the inside of you! Pick up your Bible, God's training manual. Talk to the Holy Ghost. The Holy Ghost is waiting to guide you and to answer your questions. He is ready to take you into a place where you can express that potential that is inside of you.

Are you ready to reign? Before you close this book, I want you to say one more time, *"I am not going to leave this earth with all this potential inside of me. Lord, help me to fully express who you made me to be starting right now. Let Your kingdom come in my life here on earth as it is in heaven."* Now, get ready to experience what it means to reign in this life through Christ our King.

About the Author

William (Bill) Samuel Winston

Bill Winston is a visionary founder and senior pastor of **Living Word Christian Center** in Forest Park, Illinois. He is also founder and president of **Bill Winston Ministries**, a partnership-based global outreach ministry that shares the gospel through television, radio, and the internet; the nationally accredited **Josheph Business School** which has partnership locations on five continents and an online program; the **Living**

Word School of Ministry and Missions; and Faith Ministries Alliance (FMA), an organization of more than 800 churches and ministries under his spiritual covering in the United States and other countries.

The ministry owns and operates two shopping malls, **Forest Park Plaza** in Forest Park and **Washington Plaza** in Tuskegee, Alabama.

Bill is married to Veronica and is the father of three, Melody, Allergra, and David, and the grandfather of eight.

Books by Bill Winston

- Be My Witness
- Born Again and Spirit-Filled
- Climbing Without Compromise
- Divine Favor – A Gift from God, Expanded Edition
- Faith and the Marketplace: Becoming the Person of Influence God Intended You to Be
- Faith in the Blessing
- Imitate God and Get Results
- Possessing Your Mountain
- Power of the Tongue
- Seeding for the Billion Flow
- Supernatural Wealth Transfer: Restoring the Earth to Its Rightful Owners
- Tapping the Wisdom of God
- The God Kind of Faith, Expanded Edition

• The Kingdom of God in You: Releasing the Kingdom, Replenishing the Earth
• The Law of Confession: Revolutionize Your Life and Rewrite Your Future with the Power of Words
• The Missing Link of Meditation
• The Power of Grace
• The Power of the Tithe
• The Spirit of Leadership: Leadership Lessons Learned from the Life of Joseph
• Training for Reigning: Releasing the Power of Your Potential
• Transform Your Thinking, Transform Your Life: Radically Change Your Thoughts, Your World, and Your Destiny
• Vengeance of the Lord: The Justice System of God

Some books are available in other languages.

IF YOU'RE A FAN OF THIS BOOK, PLEASE TELL OTHERS...

- Write about *Training for Reigning: Releasing the Power of Your Potential* on your blog, Twitter, and Facebook page.

- Suggest *Training for Reigning: Releasing the Power of Your Potential* to friends.

- This book is available through all major distributors, so any bookstore that does not have *Training for Reigning: Releasing the Power of Your Potential* in stock can easily order it.

- Write a positive review of *Training for Reigning: Releasing the Power of Your Potential* on www.amazon.com.

- Send my publisher, HigherLife Publishing, suggestions on Web sites, conferences, and events you know of where this book could be offered at info@ahigherlife.com.

- Purchase additional copies to give away as gifts.

CONNECT WITH US!

Connect with Bill Winston Ministries
on Social Media
Visit www.billwinston.org/social to connect
with all our official Social Media channels

Bill Winston Ministries
P.O. Box 947
Oak Park, Illinois 60303-0947
(708) 697-5100
(800) 711-9327
www.billwinston.org

Bill Winston Ministries Africa
22 Salisbury Road
Morningside, Durban, KWA Zulu Natal 4001
+27(0)313032541 orders@billwinston.org.za
www.billwinston.org.za

Bill Winston Ministries Canada
P.O. Box 2900
Vancouver BC V6B 0L4
(844) 298-2900
www.billwinston.ca

Prayer Call Center
(877) 543-9443